'S OF THINGS ARE GOIN ON NOW THAT DIDN'T USETER

FARMER AND HE CAN'T GET A FARM ★ THAT DROUGHT

NG COME AND FOUND US BLANK ★ HERE'S WHAT I THINK ON IT—THE TRAC-

FROM DAWN TILL YOU JUST CAN'T SEE ★ THE MONEY MEN GOT THAT COUN-

HE COUNTRY IS THE BIG LANDOWNERS ★ THE FARMALL IS KNOCKING OUR

TOP TO SHUT THE DOOR THEY JUST WALK OUT ★ HE CLAIMS TRACTORS IS

AND BUY FARMALLS ★ WE CAN WORK THIS LAND AS GOOD AS ANYBODY. WE

RED TELL OF THIS HERE IRRIGATION, PLENTY OF WATER AND PLENTY TO EAT

HE'S GOT THE OREGON ITCH ★ SON TO FATHER: YOU DIDN'T KNOW THE

VE FOR BREAKFAST ★ THIS IS A HARD LIFE TO SWALLOW BUT I JUST COULDN'T

MAKES A BUM OUT OF YOU. YOU GET STARTED AND YOU CAN'T STOP ★ MAKIN

KE TO STARVE TO DEATH ★ NIGH TO NOTHIN AS EVER I SEE ★ BURNED OUT,

STRANDED ★ I WOULDN'T HAVE RELIEF NO WAY IT WAS FIXED ★ IF YOU

T BETTER ★ LOTS OF EM HARP ABOUT THE WPA RELIEF. BUT THE BIG PLOW-UP

O BE WHITE FOLKS. WE DON'T WANT NO RELIEF. BUT WHAT WE DO WANT IS A

HY DIDN'T YOU STAY THERE—WHEN I SAYS I COME FROM TEXAS ★ WHEN YOU

SEE WHICH GITS IT ★ YOU EAT IT UP FASTER THAN YOU CAN MAKE IT ★ I

THIS LIFE IS SIMPLICITY BOILED DOWN ★ A PICTURE OF ME CAIN'T DO NO

TROUBLES WITHOUT GOING COMMUNIST ★ CHRIST I'LL DIE BEFORE I'LL SAY

WELL AND SUCH AS THAT, BUT I NEVER HAVE WROTE THAT WE LIVE IN A TENT

VE DIDN'T WANT NO RELIEF ★ WHEN THEY GET THROUGH WORKING YOU THEY

I FOUGHT AND I'M PROUD OF IT THINKIN I WAS HELPIN THE GOVERNMENT AND

AIN'T HARDLY FAIR. THEY HOLLER THAT WE AIN'T CITIZENS BUT THEIR FRUIT

OTTON OR STARVE. ★ BROTHER, HIT'S PICK SEVENTY-FIVE CENT COTTON OR

TO FIGHT NO MATTER WHERE THEY WAS. I DON'T SEE WHY WE CAN'T BE

A HUMAN BEING HAS A RIGHT TO STAND LIKE A TREE HAS A RIGHT TO STAND

American Farmers
and
The Rise of Agribusiness

Seeds of Struggle

American Farmers
and
The Rise of Agribusiness

Seeds of Struggle

Advisory Editors

Dan C. McCurry
Richard E. Rubenstein

An American Exodus

A RECORD OF HUMAN EROSION

BY

Dorothea Lange & Paul Schuster Taylor

ARNO PRESS

A New York Times Company

New York — 1975

Reprint Edition 1975 by Arno Press Inc.

AMERICAN FARMERS AND THE RISE OF AGRIBUSINESS:
Seeds of Struggle
ISBN for complete set: 0-405-06760-7
See last pages of this volume for titles.

Manufactured in the United States of America

◆▶

Library of Congress Cataloging in Publication Data

Lange, Dorothea.
    An American exodus.

    (American farmers and the rise of agribusiness)
    Reprint of the ed. published by Reynal & Hitchcock,
New York.
    1. Agricultural laborers--United States--Pictorial
works. 2. Migration, Internal--United States--Picto-
rial works. 3. Depressions--1929--United States--Pic-
torial works. I. Taylor, Paul Schuster, 1895-
joint author. II. Title. III. Series.
HD1525.L3 1975   973.91'6'0222   74-30641
ISBN 0-405-06811-5

An
American Exodus

OLD SOUTH

PLANTATION UNDER THE MACHINE

MIDCONTINENT

PLAINS

DUST BOWL

LAST WEST

An American Exodus

A RECORD OF HUMAN EROSION

BY

Dorothea Lange & Paul Schuster Taylor

REYNAL & HITCHCOCK

NEW YORK

FOREWORD:

EXODUS from the land is not new. Since the Middle Ages in Europe an unending stream of rural folk has fed the growth of cities and furnished manpower for rising manufactures. In America throughout our national history people have migrated in a double stream. One current, itself a part of the 500-year old stream of Europe, has drawn off surplus population from land already settled in order to urbanize and industrialize the United States. The other current, described a century ago by the Frenchman de Toqueville, has moved steadily westward with "the solemnity of a providential event . . . like a deluge of men rising unabatedly, and daily driven onward by the hand of God." Its goal was a piece of unoccupied domain for each family to assure a living through tillage of the soil.

The generation of our fathers saw the end of the western frontier of free land. And it is now a full decade since the doors of our factories were open wide to boys from the farms. Indeed, in the face of industrial collapse in 1929 millions of Americans sought refuge in recoil to the land from which they had sprung. . . . Now our people are leaving the soil again. They are being expelled by powerful forces of man and of Nature. They crowd into cities and towns near the plantations. Once more great numbers of landseekers trek west.

This contemporary exodus is our theme. It attains its most dramatic form on the deltas, the prairies, and the plains of the South, and in the tide of people which moves to the Pacific Coast. But this time the cities and towns are already burdened with unemployed, and opportunity upon the land is sharply restricted.

This is neither a book of photographs nor an illustrated book, in the traditional sense. Its particular form is the result of our use of tech-

5

niques in proportions and relations designed to convey understanding easily, clearly, and vividly. We use the camera as a tool of research. Upon a tripod of photographs, captions, and text we rest themes evolved out of long observations in the field. We adhere to the standards of documentary photography as we have conceived them. Quotations which accompany photographs report what the persons photographed said, not what we think might be their unspoken thoughts. Where there are no people, and no other source is indicated, the quotation comes from persons whom we met in the field.

We show you what is happening in selected regions of limited area. Something is lost by this method, for it fails to show fully the wide extent and the many variations of rural changes which we describe. But we believe that the gain in sharpness of focus reveals better the nature of the changes themselves.

In this work of collaboration it is not easy nor perhaps important to weigh the separate contributions of each author. Those distinctions which are clearest arise from the fact that this rural scene was viewed together by a photographer and a social scientist. All photographs, with the few exceptions indicated, were taken by Dorothea Lange. Responsibility for the text rests with Paul Taylor. Beyond that, our work is a product of cooperation in every aspect from the form of the whole to the least detail of arrangement or phrase.

Our work has produced the book, but in the situations which we describe are living participants who can speak. Many whom we met in the field vaguely regarded conversation with us as an opportunity to tell what they are up against to their government and to their countrymen at large. So far as possible we have let them speak to you face to face. Here we pass on what we have seen and learned from many miles of countryside of the shocks which are unsettling them.

DOROTHEA LANGE
PAUL SCHUSTER TAYLOR

Berkeley, California
August 1, 1939

Old South

THE EMPIRE OF COTTON
NOW STRETCHES FROM THE ATLANTIC TO THE PACIFIC

HOE CULTURE

Alabama, 1937

ONE MULE, SINGLE PLOW

"The South is an agricultural area in the midst of an industrialized nation."—RUPERT B. VANCE

Eutah, Alabama. July 1, 1937

"The South is poor, the land is poor, the only crop is cotton, the houses are without paint, weeds crowd up to the door, the tenants are ill-clad. . . ."—RUPERT B. VANCE

Alabama, 1937

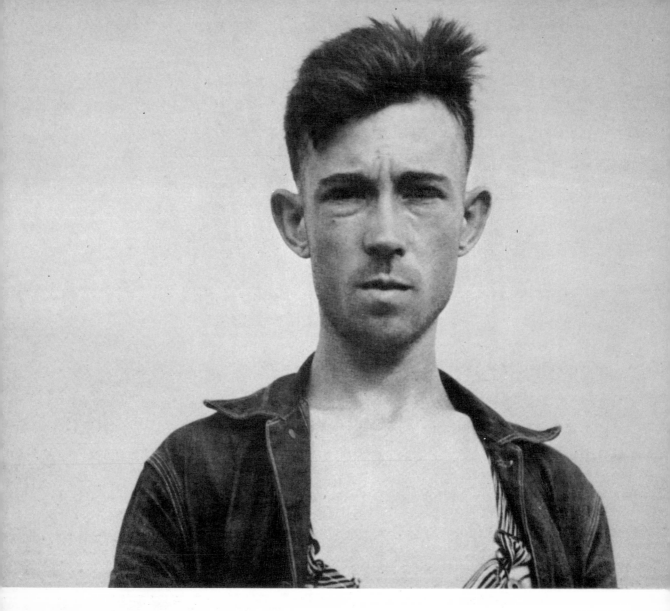

YOUNG SHARECROPPER ON $5 A MONTH "FURNISH"

"Hit's a hard get-by. The land's just fit fer to hold the world together. We think the landlord ought to let the government have this land and build it up, but he's got money and he don't believe in that way. Between Buck Creek and Whitewater Creek nobody can make a living."

NEIGHBOR: "A piece of meat in the house would like to scare these children of mine to death."

Macon County, Georgia, July 16, 1937

COUPLE, BORN IN SLAVERY

"I remember when the Yankees come through, a whole passel of 'em, hollerin', and told the Negroes you're free. But they didn't get nothin' 'cause we had carried the best horses and mules over to the gulley."

Plantation with 28 families abandoned in 1924 after the boll weevil struck.

Greene County, Georgia. July 20, 1937

AGRICULTURAL LADDER

"The Committee's examination of the agricultural ladder has indicated
. . . an increasing tendency for the rungs of the ladder to become bars
—forcing imprisonment in a fixed social status from which it is increas-
ingly difficult to escape."

President's Committee on Farm Tenancy. 1937

16

"The collapse of the plantation system, rendered inevitable by its exploitation of land and labor, leaves in its wake depleted soil, shoddy livestock, inadequate farm equipment, crude agricultural practices, crippled institutions, a defeated and impoverished people."

—ARTHUR F. RAPER

Lower Piedmont, Greene County, Georgia. July 1937

OLD SOUTH: Although we have nearly for-

gotten it, the spread across the South of a vigorous rural structure which now we call a problem was itself the product of a machine invented barely five generations ago. Planted by the earliest English settlements in America, cotton served little more than the domestic uses of house-holds throughout the colonial era. Not until the slow, laborious, hand method of separating closely-adhering lint from cottonseed could be mechanized, was commercial production feasible.

In 1793 the Yankee Whitney invented the saw gin. The effect was immediate. Cotton production doubled in four years and increased eight-fold during the decade ending in 1804. There were no limits to the expanding market, for inventions in Great Britain were revolu-tionizing the textile industry and beginning to clothe the world in machine-made cotton cloth. In America slavery became more profitable.

In the Piedmont from Georgia to Virginia men grew more cotton.

By 1825 planters and their slaves were beginning to settle Alabama, the Lower Mississippi, the Red River Valley in Louisiana, and western Tennessee. By 1860 the center of gravity of southern cotton production already had moved west along the Black Belt in Alabama on to the delta lands of the Mississippi, and the fringes of the Cotton Belt lay across Arkansas and eastern Texas.

As the planters advanced westward through the forests they established the basic characteristics of the Cotton Belt. They settled on the choicest lands of the South. They reared a landed aristocracy. They developed a one-crop economy and laid the southern foundations of a sectionalism which split the nation in the War between the States.

On the ruins of War the sharecropper replaced the slave. Neither planter nor laborer could readily command credit. So the propertyless freedman took his pay in a share of the crop instead of wages, and he mortgaged that share for the advances of subsistence "furnished" him by the planter while the crop matured. Thus, despite scattered protests by southern farmers in the late sixties that the sharecrop system was "a ruinous one to the interests of the country and its labor" it became riveted on the South.

Rural poverty in cotton is no longer a problem of race. After the War white workers began to engage in the production of cotton which previously they had shunned. Today after less than three generations white sharecroppers are almost equal in number to black sharecroppers, and as tenants they outnumber the colored by nearly two to one.

Nor does exhaustion of the soil distinguish the color of its victims. As in the North the pioneers were wasteful of the land. Even before the War a southern Congressman complained of Alabama "fields once fertile, now unfenced, abandoned and covered with those evil harbingers, fox-tail and broomsedge. . . . Indeed, a country in its infancy, where, fifty years ago, scarce a forest tree had been felled by the axe of the pioneer, is already exhibiting the painful signs of senility and decay apparent in Virginia and the Carolinas." Erosion, boll weevil, lost markets have forced plantation mansions into decay and left undernourished families on impoverished land.

The rural problems of the lower strata in the South are deeply rooted in the past. They have developed in the society created by cotton. They focus largely on masses of poor or propertyless workers, white and black, using simple methods of production in the fields, with little opportunity to rise.

Plantation Under the Machine

DELTA OF THE MISSISSIPPI

"Cotton obsessed, Negro obsessed, and flood ridden, it is the deepest South, the heart of Dixie, America's super-plantation belt. The Delta . . . consists of a series of basins of rivers . . . in Arkansas . . . in Mississippi . . . in Louisiana . . . Together with the alluvial lands of the great river, these basins form the Delta."—RUPERT B. VANCE

Cotton plantation in Arkansas Delta.

August 1938

"Nowhere are ante bellum conditions so nearly preserved as in the Yazoo Delta."—RUPERT B. VANCE

Yazoo Delta, Mississippi. August 1938

The Delta is the most concentrated cotton-growing section of the deep South. Land holdings are large, and on each 12 to 15 acres of this crop lives a tenant or sharecropper family. The countryside was deliberately populated densely in order to make available on the plantation itself enough hands to meet peak requirements for hand pickers at harvest.

Pulaski County in the Arkansas Bottoms. June 1938

MECHANIZATION IS INVADING THE DELTA WITH DEVELOPMENT OF THE
PNEUMATIC-TIRED, ALL-PURPOSE TRACTOR

On this plantation only 30 families remain to work at day labor where
160 sharecropper families lived on the land. Twenty-two tractors and
13 four-row cultivators have replaced 130 families.

Near Greenville, Mississippi. June 1937

New and Old Elements in the Landscape

Tractor and plantation cabin.

Arkansas Delta. August 1938

Old Forms Remain, but They are Changed at the Core

Day labor family on a plantation; formerly sharecroppers.

On U S 61 Arkansas Delta. Saturday afternoon, August 1938

Cotton workers, swept from the land, fill the towns. From crowded slums they are daily drawn back to the plantations to hoe and to pick cotton in seasons when they are needed. At the bridgehead, 5 a.m., bound for a day's work on the Arkansas delta. Wages 90 cents to $1.25 a day.

Memphis, Tennessee, June 1937

LINE-UP OF NEGRO UNEMPLOYED AT THE STATE EMPLOYMENT SERVICE

Memphis, Tennessee. June 1938

ABANDONED TENANT CABIN IN THE MISSISSPPI DELTA. 1937

"They ain't nothin' but day labor . . .
Right smart empty houses on that place . . .
Heap of 'em go far places."

AN AGRICULTURAL EXPERIMENT STATION
RECOMMENDS—

"MAKING COTTON CHEAPER"
"CAN PRESENT PRODUCTION COSTS BE REDUCED?"

"From 30 to 50 percent of present Delta farm labor must ultimately be replaced by machinery if plantations are to escape foreclosure. . . .

Putting labor on a cash or day basis will increase its efficiency 50 to 100 percent.

As cultivating machinery is improved, more hoeing can be eliminated by cross plowing. Cotton-chopping machines will also assist. . . .

Soap box orators may decry cotton pickers, tractors, two- and four-mule machinery but they and other modern farm machines are just as essential to farmers who expect to earn decent livings and fair returns on investments as are linotypes to printers, compressed air and concrete-mixing machines to contractors, modern spinning and weaving machines to textile manufacturers, or modern equipment to other American industries. . . . It is not up to American farms to absorb, even at pauper wages, either the labor released from modernized industry or non-essential farm labor replaced by the economical use of adapted farm machines."

Bulletin 298. Delta Experiment Station. 1932

Hoers going back to work after lunch on a Mississippi Delta plantation.
Part of day-labor gang hauled by truck out of Clarksdale.

June 1937

More Men Than Jobs at the Bridgehead Labor Market

"They come off the plantations 'cause they ain't got nothin' to do. . . .
They come to town and they *still* got nothin' to do."

Memphis, Tennessee. June 1938

"The country's in an uproar now—it's in bad shape. The people's all leaving the farm. You can't get anything for your work, and everything you buy costs high. Do you reckon I'd be out on the highway if I had it good at home?"

On US 80 near El Paso. June 1938

THE QUESTION ARISES—

"I say: A rollin' stone gathers no moss.
He says: A settin' hen never gets fat.
I say to him: Better stay here where people know us.
We'd have to sell our team and maybe we'd be left flatfooted.
I know about 15 families from Senath that's gone to California.
Some of 'em made out and some of 'em didn't."

Southeast Missouri. August 7, 1938

FAMILY COMING FROM TOWN ON SATURDAY AFTERNOON. DELTA OF
THE MISSISSIPPI

Southeast Missouri. August 1938

Evicted Sharecroppers Camp Along Highways In Missouri

Plantations of the Delta are coming under the machine. The sharecropper system is collapsing at its advance, and croppers are being cut from the land. In protest, hundreds of families—white and black victims of its devastation—left their cabins in January 1939 to camp along 150 miles of open road.

Highway US 61 in southeast Missouri

PLANTATION UNDER THE MACHINE:

On the alluvial lands of the Mississippi River and its tributaries the plantation system reached its fullest development. By 1810 in the cotton parishes of the Louisiana delta slaves already were from 55 to 63 percent of the total population. By 1840 in Bolivar and Issaquena counties of the Yazoo-Mississippi delta where settlement was retarded by floods, 72 percent of the population were slaves. At the outbreak of the War between the States 89 percent of the total population in that area were slaves, a proportion approached in the Cotton Belt only across the river in delta parishes of Louisiana.

Not only did the proportion of slave to free population approximate nine to one in sections of the delta, but the concentration of slaves held by each cotton plantation was the highest in the South. In 1860 when the average holding of slaves ranged from 17 to 47 in the older upland cotton areas of the Southeast, from 10 to 49 in upland areas of Alabama and Mississippi, and from 16 to 29 in upland regions west of the River, the average reached 55 in the Yazoo delta, 117 in Concordia Parish of the Louisiana delta, 118 in Issaquena County, Mississippi, and 125 in Rapides Parish in the Arkansas Valley.

Since Emancipation large plantations have survived more vigorously in the delta than anywhere in the Cotton Belt, with sharecropping and tenancy substituted for slavery as their foundation. Today about 85 percent of the farm land is operated in plantations; the largest in the world is in Bolivar County. In county after county of the delta in Mississippi and Louisiana the colored farm population still outnumbers the white by four and five to one, and even more. Only on the alluvial lands of southeast Missouri and adjacent Arkansas delta where cotton production developed late after the Civil War do whites on the land outnumber the blacks.

Methods of producing cotton have remained primitive in the delta. One Negro behind one mule drawing a simple cultivator down long rows is still the common sight. Hoeing and picking are by hand as they were in 1793. Many hands are needed for chopping in late Spring and many more are needed for picking in early Fall. But plowing, planting, and cultivating require few workers, and between seasons and in winter there is idleness. To meet the heavy seasonal demands the plantations were drenched with laborers, and large families were encouraged. Then, since labor was ample, cheap, and must be supported anyway, there was slight incentive for more progressive methods of tillage.

But a series of changes during the 1930's is dealing the old system a series of heavy blows—a collapse in the price of cotton, the plow-up of cotton and curtailment of acreage to stiffen prices with government checks to farm operators who cooperate, a national program of public relief, and finally, perfection of the all-purpose, row-crop tractor. Faced with bankruptcy and loss of their plantations, landlords have begun to question the paternalism which since slavery has laid upon them the responsibility of caring for their people from one crop to the next. Under economic pressure they are yielding, and relief makes it easier to yield. More and more they throw the care of their workers between crops upon the public, and let their people drift to the towns. Mechanization accelerates the process, for one man with tractor and four-row tillage equipment can do the work of eight mules and eight Negroes.

The record of power farming in cutting cotton workers from the land is already impressive. A pattern of mobile labor is developing. The landless cotton worker's year is being divided into occasional employment by the day on the plantations between May and December, and virtual idleness on relief in the towns from December to May.

This problem, originating in the South, is national in its repercussions. In January 1939 more than a thousand persons, white and black, encamped in the open along the highways of southeastern Missouri and the Arkansas delta in protest against the changes on the plantations of which they are the victims. Already whites from this section are picking cotton in Arizona and peas in California. Negroes in small numbers follow the well-worn channels cut by earlier migrations to the North. No tide of blacks has yet started west.

HEARD IN THE DELTA, 1937

STATE OFFICIAL, MEMPHIS:

"Modern efficiency has hit the farms like everywhere else. Since the twenties the banks and loan companies have more and more been interested in the plantations. The banks, loan companies, and business men figure costs on the farms. They say, 'Why maintain a nigger the year around when they need him only a few months?' It's simpler to let 'em go and cut down overhead. They buy tractors, and the tenants and croppers come to the cities and we put them on relief. More and more they drive them into town and then want them back only for day labor."

NEGRO EX-CROPPER, NOW TRACTOR DRIVER AT $1.50 A DAY, ARKANSAS DELTA:

"Most every farm—most every big farm—in this country has tractors on it. For the owners hit's good, but for the tenants this is much worser."

PLANTER WHO USES TRACTORS AND DAY LABOR, ISSAQUENA COUNTY:

"There were 34 tenant families on this plantation until 1935. Now I have 11 families all on day labor. When they get organized the way they are starting to organize a union up in Arkansas, they won't be no more tenants unless they reduce their shares from halves to thirds. They'll use tractors."

TOWN NEGRO, GREENVILLE, MISSISSIPPI:

"Tractors are against the black man. Every time you kill a mule you kill a black man. You've heard about the machine picker? That's against the black man, too."

OFFICIAL OF TENANT FARMERS' UNION:

"The causes of the present situation are mechanization and large-scale ownership, the government checks, and relief. The big farmers are changing to day labor. Then they don't have to feed their families. They can bring labor from town to work by the day, and they can collect the entire government rental themselves. The AAA contract says the landowner can't cut his tenants to day labor, but after the contract is signed they *put* them on day labor. That's what started the union—the fight to get half of the check."

SHARECROPPER:

"These things are a pressin' on us in the State of Mississippi."

Midcontinent

RACE FOR CLAIMS AT THE OPENING OF THE CHEROKEE OUTLET. 1893

"Oklahoma was settled on the run by a white pioneer yeomanry."

—RUPERT B. VANCE

1867—Cattle on the Chisholm Trail
1889—"Boomers" and "sooners" rush for homesteads
1905—Oil
1907—Statehood

"I'm goin' where the climate fits my clothes. . . ."

Line from an old Oklahoma folk-song

"as to hard times, I believe the sixth chapter of Hosea, the thirty-second chapter of Deuteronomy, and the thirtieth chapter of Jeremiah apply to us in this day. When we return unto God, things will be changed for us. Work is scarce here, with many on the relief rolls and WPA work."

Oklahoma reader to Dallas Farm News. February 7, 1939

There are Many Small Cotton Farms in Eastern Oklahoma

On US 62 August 10, 1938

MAN AND WIFE, WITH FIVE CHILDREN—

"There's lots of ways to break a man down. In 1934 I give a year's work for $56.16 sharecropping 16 acres of bottom land in Love County, Texas. Had to leave 4 to 6 bales of cotton standing in the field, with not a mattress in the house and we couldn't gin our own cotton to make one. I got my brother-in-law to give me the money to get the gas to bring me back from Love County."

—$26.40 A MONTH (WPA) HOLDS MANY A FAMILY IN OKLAHOMA

On 40 acres of Black Jack and Post Oak, cultivating 7.

Near Henryetta, eastern Oklahoma. August 10, 1938

THE DUST OF THEIR EARLIER MIGRATION HAD NOT SETTLED BEFORE
NEW MIGRATIONS BEGAN

Oklahomans on U S 99 in the San Joaquin Valley of California.

April 16, 1938

FAMILIES MILL AROUND—

"We're bound for Kingfisher, Oklahoma, to work in the wheat, and Lubbock, Texas, to work in the cotton. We're trying not to, but we'll be in California yet."

> *Family with 7 children from Paris, Arkansas, on the highway near Webber Falls, Oklahoma. June 27, 1938*

WANT AD SCOPE!

Perhaps no other single medium is so far-reaching, or serves in such a multitude of capacities as does the want ads. From the cradle to the end of life's span, Oklahoman and Times Want Ads are daily benefactors ... serving the individual in all his daily needs regardless of size or importance. The most trivial want as well as life's most important venture find realization through the Oklahoman and Times Want Ads.

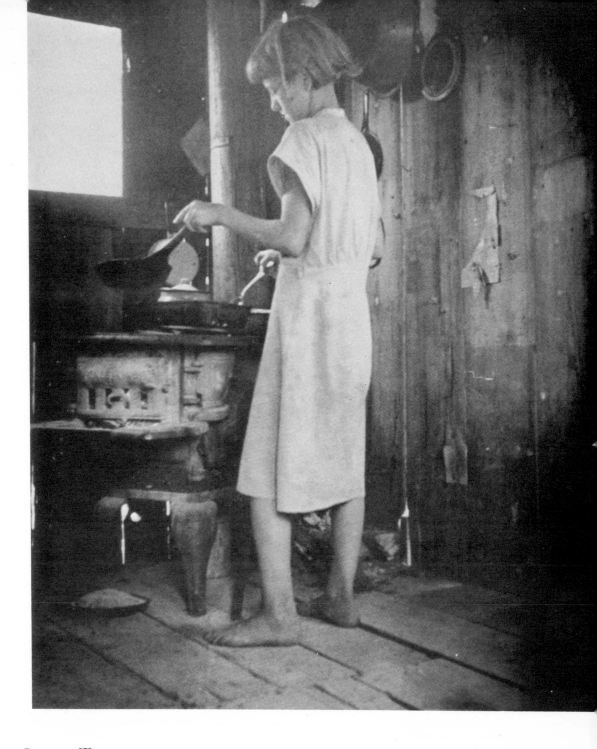

SUPPER TIME

On "Highway No. 1 of the OK State." August 1936

"I'VE TURNED FOUR HORSES ABREAST MANY A DAY"

Oklahoma County, Oklahoma. August 12, 1938

THROUGH OKLAHOMA STREAM EMIGRANTS FROM KANSAS, MISSOURI, ARKANSAS—WESTBOUND

"They're goin' every direction and they don't know where they're goin'."—FARMER

Hitch-hiking from Joplin, Missouri, to a sawmill job in Arizona. On U S 66 near Weatherford, western Oklahoma.

August 12, 1938

"We started from Joplin, Missouri, with $5. We're bound for California if we can make it in time for grape picking."

Muskogee, Oklahoma. June 27, 1938

DROUGHT OF 1936

"I seen our corn dry up and blow over the fence, back there in Oklahoma," said a pea picker in California in February, 1937.

RETURNING FROM CALIFORNIA—

"People aren't friendly there like they are here, but they appreciate the cheap labor coming out. When there's a rush for work they're friendlier than at other times."

Canadian County, Oklahoma. August 1938

—RETURNED

"Whole families go to Los Angeles, Phoenix, Bakersfield.
Half the people of this town and around here have gone out there."

—*Said at the drug store*

Also many come back, like this family just home from California.

Muskogee County, Oklahoma. August 10, 1938

Agricultural Depression, Years of Drought, Depopulation

Caddo, Oklahoma. June 16, 1938

No Rain

Stricken farmers, idle in town during the great drought.

Sallisaw, Oklahoma. August 1936

Homeless family, tenant farmers in 1936. Cut from the land by illness, driven to the road by poverty, they walk from county to county in search of the meagre security of relief.

Atoka County, Oklahoma. June 16, 1938

HIGHWAY TO THE WEST

"They keep the road hot a goin' and a comin'."
"They've got roamin' in their head."

U S 54 in southern New Mexico

MIDCONTINENT:

"They're goin' to California like they used to go to Michigan. I'm a slow-movin' feller—California is too fast fer me."

Walnut Ridge, Arkansas. August 7, 1938

"Everyone writes back he's heeled. He's got him a job."

Arkansas. August, 1938

"Ain't it a fright—how they're a goin'. Sleepin' out there on the sand in any kind of a miserable way! My neighbor over yonder to the south has got two boys and a girl out there, and my neighbor over thataway on the north section, he's got a son gone out there, but he's writin' on comin' back the 14th of next month." *Oklahoma. August 10, 1938*

Letter from county welfare office of LeFlore County, Oklahoma, to a county relief administrator in California, Feb. 2, 1938:

"In the past I have authorized the return of a goodly number of families from your state, and after they paid a short visit to their relatives and friends, they all returned to California, with one exception. In view of this fact I feel that it is an imposition upon your state as well as a burden on myself to investigate these cases and authorize return from which it seems, that in all cases, it is just for a visit."

The roots of Oklahomans in the land are shallow. The first of a series of openings which signalized victory for land-hungry farmers outside the Territory, over Indians and cattlemen inside, took place barely a half-century ago. Rapidly thereafter the state was covered with farms. Beginning cotton production only in the middle nineties, the farmers raised their yield in a single generation to a peak of nearly 1,800,000 bales, exceeded only by Texas and Mississippi. With equal rapidity there was erected a structure of tenancy which in 1935 stood at 61 percent of all farms, and ranks with the highest in the nation. But the State has not maintained its position in cotton production, nor has its tenancy the binding qualities and stability of an old plantation system. Deposits of petroleum were discovered first in 1907, and big industrial and financial institutions were erected upon them in two decades. But the world of oil which built cities has left the realm of agriculture untouched.

The early settlers coming to Oklahoma in trainloads, recalls Thomas Benton, "were too much under the influence of the moving itch . . ." Later as tenants they exhibited the usual propensity to shift about from farm to farm. In season, they migrate to the berry fields of Arkansas, and to the wheat and cotton harvests on the Plains to the west. For a generation the labor agents for the cotton growers of Arizona and California have known that Oklahoma farm folk are among the most footloose in the country, and can be detached on the promise of seasonal work by distribution of circulars and insertion of advertisements in newspapers. By a curiously symbolic coincidence Oklahoma is the most wind-blown state in the country, its newly-broken red plains are among the worst eroded, and its farm people are among the least rooted to the soil.

Adding to its traditional unsettlement, Oklahoma shares with neighboring states the effects of protracted agricultural depression, drought, depletion of mineral resources, destruction of soils, displacement of farm workers by mechanization, and accumulation in its poorest rural sections of population rebuffed by industrial centers of the North which previously had furnished outlet. On blind sections, in the corners of national highways, on the fringes of towns, and even in sight of its great capitol which rests on oil, communities of those severed from the land and from industry have reared themselves in makeshift shelters.

Migration is in all directions. Into Oklahoma distressed people pour as through a funnel, going westward, southward, or passing back on their way to Arkansas and Missouri. California and Arizona licenses on old cars tell the many who have returned. Inquiries reveal others who go again and return again, milling back and forth, seeking opportunity over and over again in Arkansas, Texas, Arizona, New Mexico, even Florida, and above all on the Pacific Coast.

> Lord I'm goin' down the road feelin' bad . . .
> Chorus: I'm not goin' to be treated thisaway.
>
> Lord they feed me on corn bread and beans . . .
> Lord I'm goin' where the climate fits my clothes . . .
> Lord an empty match box holds my clothes . . .
> Lord where I go nobody knows . . .
> Chorus: I'm not goin' to be treated thisaway.
> *Old Oklahoma folk song*

Plains

Behind on the Delta, sharecroppers working one man to the mule raised
12 to 15 acres of cotton. On to the Plains below the cap rock pushed
yeoman farmers owning teams and tools. With four- and six-mule teams
drawing two-row outfits they found they could farm a quarter section.
This was a beginning of mechanization in cotton.

Texas 1938

But Mechanization is a Process Without End. Tractors Replace Mules

Indians	1850	Buffalo
Grass	1870	Cattle
Cotton	1895	Mules
Cotton	1935	Tractors

Texas 1938

SOUTHWESTERN FARM PAPER:

"The chief advantage of a tractor is that it can do a lot of work in a short time. . . . You can run a tractor all day—and all night too. . . . Tractors are not expensive to operate. . . . In addition . . . consider the convenience of tractors."

Childress County, Texas. June 1938

Tractors Replace Not Only Mules, but People. They Cultivate
to the Very Door of the Houses of Those Whom They Replace

Childress County, Texas. June 1938

"THAT PLACE HAS MADE A LIVING FOR A FAMILY EVER SINCE THE LAND
WAS BROKE."

Abandoned house, Texas Panhandle. June 1937

THE TREELESS LANDSCAPE IS STREWN WITH EMPTY HOUSES

Near Olustee, southwestern Oklahoma. June 21, 1938

All Displaced Tenant Farmers. The Oldest 33

All native Americans, none able to vote because of Texas poll tax. All on WPA. They support an average of four persons each on $22.80 a month.

> "Where we gonna go?"
> "How we gonna get there?"
> "What we gonna do?"
> "Who we gonna fight?"
> "If we fight, what we gotta whip?"

North Texas. Sunday morning, June 1937

"Instability and insecurity of farm families leach the binding elements of rural community life." [above]
—*President's Committee on Farm Tenancy. 1937*

North Texas. June 1937

Father born in Georgia, mother in Tennessee. Born in Johnson County, Texas. Age 70. Farmed all his life. Has four children, all farmers. 17 years on this farm, tractored out in 1939. "What will I do? I don't know. My boys? It's not a question of what they are *going* to do. It's a question of what they are going to *have* to do." [right]

Hardeman County, Texas. June 1938

LANDLORD:

"I let 'em all go. In '34 I had I reckon four renters and I didn't make anything. I bought tractors on the money the government give me and got shet o' my renters. You'll find it everywhere all over the country thataway. I did everything the government said—except keep my renters. The renters have been having it this way ever since the government come in. They've got their choice—California or WPA."

—Displaced Tenant:

"The whole works of us is in it right now. The people ain't got no say a comin'."

Cross-roads filling station, southwestern Oklahoma. June 21, 1938

TRACTORED OUT ON JANUARY 1, 1938, he says:

"I can count 23 farmers in the west half of this county that have had to leave the farms to give three men more land."

"Was waiting to see what would be the outcome of my hunt for a place, and the outlook right now is that I will move to town and sell my teams, tools, and cows. I have hunted from Childress, Texas, to Haskell, Texas, a distance of 200 miles, and the answer is the same."

"I can stay off the relief until the first of the year. After that I don't know. I've got to make a move, but I don't know where to."

Texas Plains. June 20, 1938

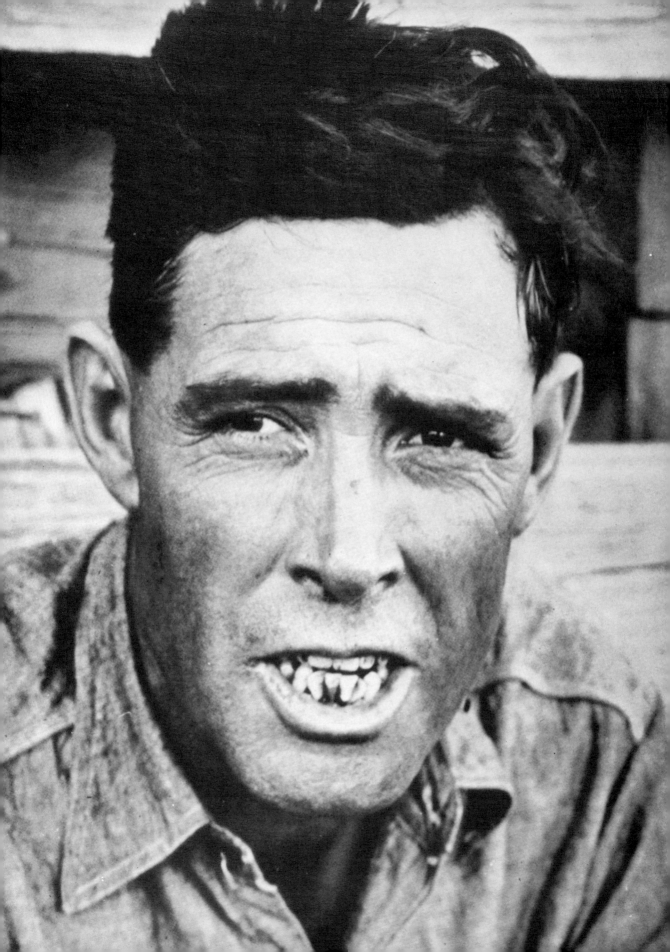

WESTWARD TO THE PACIFIC COAST ON U S 80

"They've gone west and such as that. First one place and then another."
"Since '34, that's when it went to startin'. Each year they keep turning
'em out."

New Mexico. 1938

PLAINS:

THE foundations of plantation society were laid firmly before the Civil War on the river bottoms. The opportunity of yeoman farmers came a full generation after the War, on the plains. Beyond the Black Wax Prairie of Texas gently undulating grass lands invited the farmer to move west. Land could be had cheap from the cattlemen. On the plains was no established order with rigid social classes, nor any stigma holding labor suited only to freedmen. Soil was virgin, topography was adapted to the most progressive methods of tillage, and the export market still was calling for more cotton.

By the middle nineties sturdy communities of working farmers were producing cotton in the southeastern Panhandle, and building a democracy as evenly based as the surface of their land. These white pioneer yeomen either owned their farms or, more commonly, as tenants they owned teams and tools, feed and seed. They farmed on thirds and fourths—a third of the feed to the landlord and a fourth of the cotton—not on halves like propertyless sharecroppers in the delta. They adopted the highest ratios of power per man, driving four- and six-mule teams, with two-row tillage machinery. They sought the largest amount of land per family, expanding cotton acreage from the 12 to 15 customary on the delta to between 75 and 100 on the plains. For the harvest they relied on the migration of Mexicans from south Texas 400 miles away. When labor was scarce and the crop heavy in the late twenties they introduced sleds to mechanize the harvest.

With the thirties came long depression. Between 1931 and 1933 the farm price index of cotton and cottonseed stood at the unprecedentedly low points of 63, 47, and 63 percent of the pre-war base. On the plains this same decade also brought drought. In Hall and Childress counties of the Panhandle the average ginnings which stood at 99,000 bales in the late twenties were dropped to less than half by crop failures in the thirties. In the worst years ginnings collapsed to 12,500 bales in 1934 and 26,500 in 1936. Taxes on the land went unpaid, owners lost their farms through foreclosure, and tenants despairing of a crop and laborers of employment began to leave the farms, move to town on relief, and emigrate to other parts.

The process of displacement from the land started by depression and drought, now is receiving impetus from the machine. Landlords in desperation who previously rented their land to tenants, and loan companies which have foreclosed, are taking over the operation of farms. Spurred by the necessity of cheaper costs of production and the desire to avoid sharing with tenants the cash payments under the agricultural adjustment program, they are shifting from operation by tenants to operation by wage labor employed by the day. And they are turning to mechanization to hold their position, as did the first settlers on the plains before them. With their mules and crop-reduction checks as down payments, landlords and a few of the stronger tenants are purchasing the newly-developed all-purpose tractor. Thus they reduce the human labor required and at the same time enlarge the size of their farms by cutting one tenant family from the land where there were two before.

The course which tenant displacement is running full tilt on the plains manifests itself clearly on the landscape, now dotted with abandoned tenants' houses, windows boarded, and fields cultivated close. On the edges of towns rural slums are rising. Village merchants lose trade and fail. Drought and depression are bad for them, but displacement is their finish. Schools shrink, teachers are dismissed, and churches languish. Mechanization of the farms and bad crops operate like good roads to the detriment of village institutions.

Alternatives for the displaced tenants are few and bitter. Many go to the towns or move into farmhouses vacated by other displaced tenants, and fall upon WPA or another form of relief. Some become wage laborers on mechanized farms, a sharp loss of status for yeoman farmers who once owned their teams and tools. Few who are displaced remain on the same farm which they have occupied as tenants. Some families go eastward in retreat to a submarginal farm, but many more go west. They sell off their possessions, buy a cheap used car and home-made trailer, load their bedding, stove and children, and emigrate to the irrigated farms of Arizona and California.

Tenants who yet retain farms are starkly fearful that they too may lose them and suffer the fate of the others. Those who have long been living at relief levels are becoming dispirited and hopeless. Open class conflict has not broken out, but elements of it are present. In protest rural folk write letters to the Dallas Farm News:

Each tractor means from one to three farmers on WPA or other government job at starvation wages. There are thousands of families that have been driven from the farms who would rather farm than do anything else, but there isn't any land to rent. Why not? The tractor farmer has rented or leased it all. (Feb. 7, 1939)

Another letter says:

Hall County now has more than 200 tractors on the farms, and shipments of new ones are received almost daily. It appears that the big landowners have gone money-mad, and, too, at the expense, misery, and suffering of the tenant farmer, his wife and little children . . .

Sit down and write or wire your Congressman and Senator, asking his hearty support of a movement which will mean the purchase of small tracts of land by the Federal Government upon which to locate these tenant farmers and their families. . . . We believe that there is sufficient land for all, and that the Supreme Ruler of the Universe never intended that a few should "hog" all the land, but that all should have land upon which to live, rear their families and enjoy the blessings of home ownership and its happy surroundings. (Jan. 19, 1937)

The tragedy of the democracy of the plains is that the displaced tenant, stripped of his farm and his property, is also stripped of his vote by the poll tax requirement of Texas. Those whose cry of distress is most anguished are ciphers politically to those who sit as representatives in Austin and Washington.

*   *   *   *   *

For three hundred years from the reigns of the Tudors to the nineteenth century English peasants were displaced intermittently by movements to enclose the common land. In 1549 Robert Kett led uprisings of "the misguided people [who] . . . took upon themselves to redress the matter and chose to themselves captains and leaders, brake open the enclosures . . . and made havoc after the manner of an open rebellion." The rebellion was suppressed and the leader hanged. Four years later in the Book of Private Prayer set out by Edward VI, there appeared in the Prayer for Landlords a plea using words from the Prophet Isaiah:

give them grace to consider . . . that they remembering the short continuance of their life, may be content with that that is sufficient, and not join house to house, nor couple land to land, to the impoverishment of other, but so behave themselves in letting out their tenements, lands, and pastures that after this life they may be received into everlasting dwelling places: through Jesus Christ our Lord. Amen.

In later centuries the victims of enclosures who lost their rights to common land proclaimed their grievance in doggerel:

> The law locks up the man or woman
> Who steals the goose from off the common;
> But leaves the greater villain loose
> Who steals the common from the goose.

In the long view of history, it has been adjudged by scholars that the economic effects of British enclosures were beneficial. Likewise scholars of the future may well take the view that mechanization on the plains enabled farmers to cut costs of production and to recapture a portion of the slipping export market. But the price of such progress in terms of social disorganization and human misery comes high on the plains, as it came high in sixteenth century Britain.

When the rains return to the plains the displaced tenants will probably not come back, for the new methods of farming leave them no place. Depopulation seems destined to be permanent. Perhaps it should be. Whether the rains come or drought continues, the westward stream of the distressed sons of the settlers will continue to be fed by victims of mechanization.

Dust Bowl

Grain Elevators, Barbed Wire, and Gang Plows on the High Plains

FACSIMILE OF REAL ESTATE ADVERTISEMENT

1925

1938—"Top o' the World" Farm and Dairy Lands 13 Years After

"Lots of 'em toughed it through until this year."

Coldwater. June 1938

1938—"Top o' the World" Farm and Dairy Lands 13 Years After

"They turned the land loose when they left."

Coldwater. June 1938

THE GREAT BLOW OF 1934

"Gently sifted with a nice precision the finest parts of our Plains soil fell upon boat decks and waves of the Atlantic far at sea. . . . In Texas, the skim milk—sand; in the midland, median particles; in Ohio, a light, unseen deposit, soon whisked away by water; and overhead, in Maryland the very cream of rich far-western soils blowing out to sea to be drowned and lost."—RUSSELL LORD

"Section after section dried up and blowed away."—Refugee in California

Dallam County, Texas. June 1937

"It's made good one time.
Of course everyone thinks maybe it'll come back."

Coldwater district, Texas. June 17, 1938

"Every dime I've got is tied up right here, and if I don't get it out I've got to drive off and leave it. Where would I go? I know what the land would do once. Maybe it will do it again."

Coldwater district, Texas. June 17, 1938

"Every deserted homestead shack is the key to some unwritten story that strikes deep."—WILSON AND BOWDEN

Oldham County, Texas Panhandle. June 1938

"No, I didn't *sell* out back there. I *give* out."—REFUGEE IN CALIFORNIA

Cimarron County, Oklahoma Panhandle. June 17, 1938

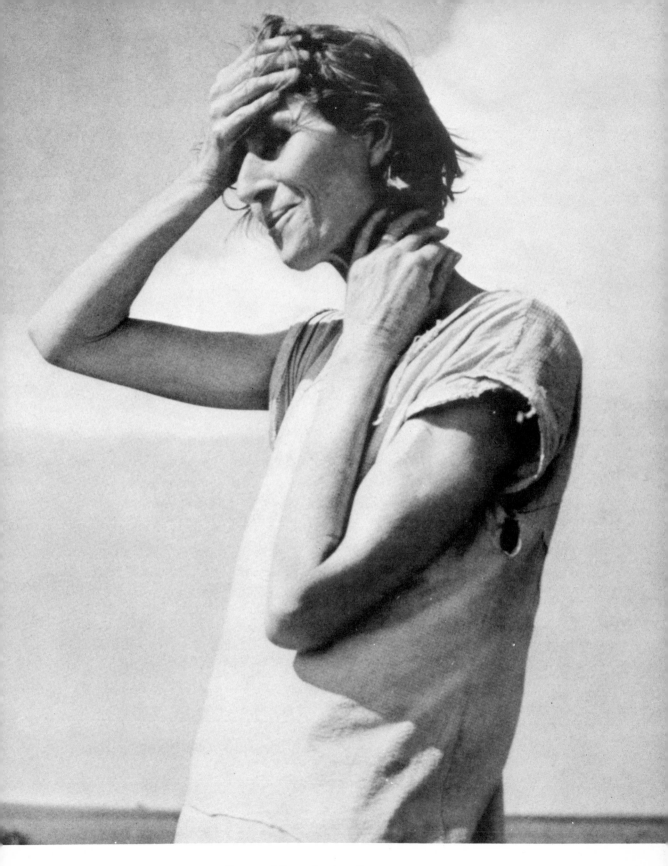

"If You Die, You're Dead—That's All"

Texas Panhandle. 1938

DUST BOWL:

LIKE fresh sores which open by over-irritation of the skin and close under the growth of protective cover, dust bowls form and heal. Dust is not new on the Great Plains, but never since man came to inhabit them has it been so pervasive and so destructive as in our decade. Dried by years of drought and pulverized by machine-drawn gang disk plows, the soil was literally thrown to the winds which whipped it in clouds across the country. The winds churned the soil, leaving vast stretches of farms blown and hummocked like deserts or the margins of beaches. They loosened the hold of settlers on the land, and like particles of dust drove them rolling down ribbons of highway.

*   *   *   *   *

Letter from a reader to the Dallas Farm News, May 16, 1939:

. . . Deer, wild turkeys, elk and buffaloes originally roamed the prairies.

Then man entered the picture with his gun and killed the buffaloes by the thousands for their hides, and left their bones to dry on the sun-bleached plains. This was the first violation of the law of nature as God intended. Years later came the long-horn cattle and sheep, with many bloody battles between cowmen and sheep ranchmen. For many years horses, cattle and sheep roamed over the prairies, grazing on the grass, the natural cover.

Then man entered with tractors and plows to break up for cultivation the millions of acres of land, plowing under the natural cover crop. As he turned the soil under he ground it into dust. Out of this came golden grains of wheat.

Then came old Mother Nature with her dust storms, in answer to Man's ruthless violations.

Then entered the Federal Government and spent millions of dollars on grass and other cover crops to restore the land as nature intended. The prairie, once the home of the deer, buffalo and antelope, is now the home of the Dust Bowl and the WPA.

I ride horseback twenty miles for my *Farm News*. If all the young folks would read your fine paper there would be less crime.

I live and "batch" alone at the wonderful Medicine Springs, in the Kiamichi Mountains, in Pushmataha County, Oklahoma. It is a very healthful resort. I would appreciate letters.

Finley, Oklahoma.

Lon Gilmore

* * * * *

"The Great Plains is a land of romance . . . of tragedy. For two and a half centuries the white man had marched westward, conquering the land. . . . On westward, into the . . . Great Plains, marched this army of settlers, but here the battle turned against them and they were thrown back by hundreds of thousands. But this battlefield of their defeat, of the triumph of their enemies is not marked by tablets, monuments, and the usual signs of victory. A lion does not write a book, nor does the weather erect a monument at the place where the pride of a woman was broken for want of a pair of shoes, or where a man worked five years in vain to build a home and gave it up, bankrupt and whipped, or where a baby died for the want of good milk, or where the wife went insane from sheer monotony and blasted hope.
—*J. Russell Smith*

* * * * *

SALUTATION IN CIMARRON COUNTY, OKLAHOMA

"Hello there Bill. What do you know for certain?"
"Nothin'."
"Well, I know it's windy and dusty. It's got so we get a half a day between the Spring Dust Storm and the Summer Dust Storm, and then we get a day and a half between the Summer Dusts and the Fall Dusts."—*August 14, 1938.*

ORIGINS OF MIGRANTS TO CALIFORNIA*

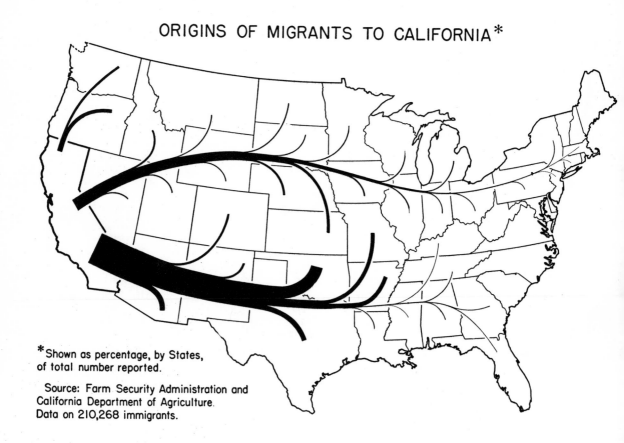

*Shown as percentage, by States,
of total number reported.

Source: Farm Security Administration and
California Department of Agriculture.
Data on 210,268 immigrants.

Last West

For three centuries an ever-receding western frontier has drawn white men like a magnet. This tradition still draws distressed, dislodged, determined Americans to our last West, hard against the waters of the Pacific.

But settlement and mechanization have transformed our frontier. The land is already occupied, and men work upon it with machines as in factories, or at hand labor in gangs as in industry.

Highways are part of the process of mechanization. Over their hard surfaces the harvested crops move in great truck-loads to market, and a labor reserve rolls in from as far east as the Mississippi to mill ceaselessly back and forth through the valleys of California following the crops. This opportunity to obtain intermittent employment in a disorganized labor market—no experience required—is our new frontier, our new West.

US 99 in the San Joaquin Valley

ENTERING CALIFORNIA THROUGH THE DESERT

Oklahoma family on US 99. March 1937

TENANT FARMER WITH SIX CHILDREN FROM COOK COUNTY, TEXAS; EN-
TERED CALIFORNIA IN 1938

"People just can't make it back there, with drought, hailstorms, wind-
storms, duststorms, insects. People exist here and they can't do that
there. You can make it here if you sleep lots and eat little, but it's pretty
tough, there are so many people. They chase them out of one camp
because they say it isn't sanitary—there's no running water—so people
live out here in the brush like a den o' dogs or pigs."

Squatters in the brush near Wasco, California. June 6, 1938

THREE FAMILIES, 14 CHILDREN

US 99, San Joaquin Valley. November 1938

"COME TO THE END OF MY ROW IN ROCKWELL COUNTY, TEXAS."

Family with 5 children left home September 1938. Picked their way across the country in Texas and Arizona cotton. Entered California the night before, and encamped along U S 80 near Holtville.

Imperial Valley. February 23, 1939

PICK PEAS FOR A CENT A POUND, 28 POUNDS TO THE HAMPER

Near Niland. February 22, 1939

GANG LABOR AND PIECE RATES IN AN OPEN-AIR FOOD FACTORY

Near Calipatria. February 22, 1939

A Carrot-tying Invention Was Tested in This Field—

"They're fixin' to free all us fellows—free us for what? Free us like they freed the mules. They're aimin' at keeping fellows such as me right down on our knees—aimin' at making slaves of us. We've got no more chance than a one-legged man in a foot-race."

Imperial Valley. February 24, 1939

Pull, Sort, Clean, and Tie for 14 Cents per Crate of 48 Bunches

"They'll sleep in the row (to hold a place in the field) to earn 60 cents a day."— A Carrot Puller

"Imperial Valley Wintergarden." February 24, 1939

Migrants in an Agricultural Labor Contractor's Camp

Nipomo. February 1936

1937—Squatter Camp on Outskirts of Holtville, Imperial Valley

150 families in squatter camp on the flats at the potato sheds. Auto licenses from Minnesota, Missouri, Oklahoma, Arizona, California, Arkansas, Texas, Nevada, Mississippi, Utah, New Mexico, Oregon, and Washington.

Edison, April 18, 1938

Auto Camp Tent Space, Water, and Electric Light $1 a Week

Tulare County. November 1938

WAITING FOR WORK ON EDGE OF THE PEA FIELDS

Waited weeks for maturity of 1937 winter crop, which froze; then more weeks until maturity of second crop.

Near Holtville. February 1937

CABINS $4 A WEEK, NO RUNNING WATER

"They're plumb full and families are doubling up."
Auto camp for migratory laborers in grapes and cotton.

Kern County. March 1937

No Work—   *Calipatria. February 25, 1937*

—Relief

The relief load rose from 188 families in November to 1,638 families in
February because a freeze ruined the early pea crop.

Crowd at relief paymaster's window, Calipatria. February 25, 1937

To Serve the Crops of California Tens of Thousands of Families
Live Literally on Wheels

Breakfast beside US 99. February 1938

One Migrant Family Hauls the Broken-down Car of the Other
to the Pea Fields at Nipomo

"Us people has got to stick together to get by these hard times."

US 101. February 21, 1936

HUNGRY BOY   *Shafter, California. November 1938*

OKLAHOMA CHILD WITH COTTON SACK READY TO GO INTO FIELD WITH
PARENTS AT 7 A.M.

Kern County, California. November 1936

OKLAHOMA FAMILY WITH 11 CHILDREN

She: "I want to go back to where we can live happy, live decent, and grow what we eat."
He: "I've made my mistake and now we can't go back. I've got nothing to farm with."

Brawley. February 23, 1939

Farmer, Left Nebraska "Monday after Easter, 1938"

"I put mine in what I thought was the best investment—the good old earth—but we lost on that, too. The finance co. caught up with us, the mortgage co. caught up with us. Managed to lose $12,000 in 3 years. My boys have no more future than I have, so far as I can see ahead."

Calipatria. February 18, 1939

Industrialized agriculture has its fullest development in California. More than one-third of all the large-scale farms of the nation are in that state.

Lettuce field. Salinas Valley. March 1939

Thirty percent of all the large-scale cotton farms in the United States
are in California (census of 1930).

Pickers empty their sacks into cotton wagon.
Near Corcoran. November 1937

Machinery prepares the ground, plants, and cultivates sugar beets. Blocking, thinning, and topping still require mobile gangs of hand laborers.

Near King City. February 1936

To perform its "stoop labor" California agriculture has drawn upon a long succession of races: Chinese, Japanese, Hindustanis, Mexicans, Filipinos, Negroes, and now American whites.

Gang of Filipino lettuce cutters. Salinas Valley. 1935

COMPANY HOUSING ON LARGE POTATO AND COTTON RANCH

Southern San Joaquin Valley. August 1938

Intensive, large-scale, and highly seasonal agriculture have created in California the largest wage-earning class, proportionately, of any important agricultural state. They have produced a large, landless, and mobile proletariat.

Near Westley. May 1938

BEGINNINGS OF ORGANIZATION

Their tap-root to the land severed, they search with their fellows where new roots may be sunk.

Migrant peach pickers. Yuba County. August 1938

COTTON PICKERS' STRIKE FAILS

Street meeting at night near the end. Kern County. November 1938 ⟶

"The Salinas strike . . . is a warning that California agriculture has outgrown its infant industrial diapers. Farming has ceased to be a simple, serene mode of living and has evolved into an outdoor factory deal, with all the attendant industrial grief."—*From "California, magazine of Pacific business." Lettuce strike, 1938*

SMALL INDEPENDENT GAS STATION DURING COTTON STRIKE

Kern County. November 1938

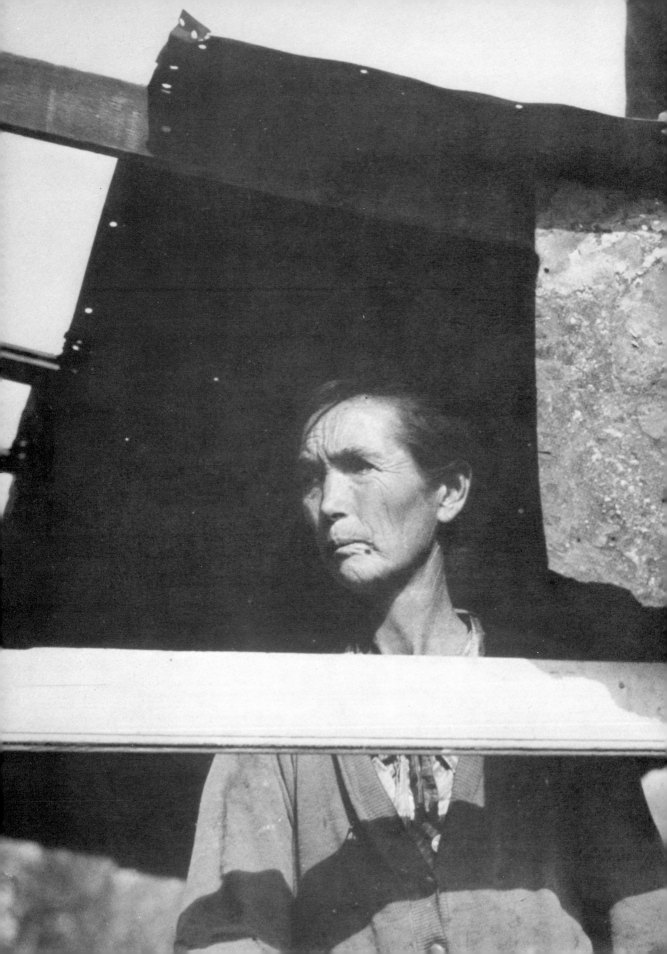

DESTINATION UNKNOWN—1939

Tens of thousands, across the country, hundreds of miles, up and down, from valley to valley, crop to crop, ranch to ranch

>"People has got to stop somewhere.
> Even a bird has got a nest."

>"We just make enough for beans, and when
> we have to buy gas it comes out of the beans."

>"What bothers us travellin' people most
> is we cain't get no place to stay still."

Kern County. November 1938

1787: DEBATE IN THE CONSTITUTIONAL CONVENTION ON LIMITING THE RIGHT OF SUFFRAGE TO FREEHOLDERS

"There is no right of which the people are more jealous than that of suffrage."—*Pierce Butler, Delegate from South Carolina*

"We ought to attend to the rights of every class of people. [I have] often wondered at the indifference of the superior classes of society to this dictate of humanity and policy, considering that, however affluent their circumstances, or elevated their situations might be, the course of a few years not only might, but certainly would, distribute their posterity throughout the lowest classes of society. Every selfish motive, therefore, every family attachment, ought to recommend such a system of policy as would provide no less carefully for the right and happiness of the lowest, than of the highest, order of citizens."—*George Mason, Delegate from Virginia*

ACTION ON THE MIGRANT PROBLEM

California's Representatives Study President's Report on State Conditions; All Agreed Solution Must Be on National Basis

BY RUTH FINNEY
The News Washington Correspondent

WASHINGTON, April 1.—During the two weeks President Roosevelt is at Warm Springs, Ga., members of the Cali-

N FRANCISCO EXAMINER: MONDAY, FEBRUARY 27, 1939

Squalor in Tent Cities

Congress

State Faces Crisis in Caring for Migrants

Idle Hordes Offer Fertile

Migrants

U.S. to Speed Relief

WASHINGTON, March 29 (P)—Office of Education and the Federal

F. R. Acts To Relieve Migrants

Orders Establishment Of Special Body to Cope With Problem

WASHINGTON, Feb. 19.— Acting on authorization given by President Roosevelt before

OLSON PROMISES TO VETO BILL PROHIBITING POOR FROM COMING INTO STATE

Governor Says American Citizens Have Constitutional Right to Travel Anywhere; Treats

BAR MIGRANTS WITH DISEASES, COUNTIES URGE

Northern Supervisors Send 'Medical Passport' System to Congress

By United Press

UBA CITY, Feb. 25—Supervis of the Alta California Area of northern counties adopted a reso ion today urging Congress to sup t a bill designed to forbid en nce to California of indigent mi nts carrying "contaminating dis-

BATTLE TO CURB MIGRANT INVASION

+++   +++   +++   +++   +++   +++

Citizens Organize Against Horde's Influx

cccc   THE SAN FRANCISCO EXAMINER: THURSDAY, MARCH

Communists' Conquest Over Migrants Stirs Californians

Okies' Camp
VOTE GROWS

ASSOCIATED FARMERS ANSWER

· · ·   · · ·   · · ·

Reply to Dispatch on Committee

100 Cotton Strikers Jailed at Bakersfield

The San Francisco News

LEAN TIME AHEAD FOR MIGRANTS

LAST WEST: Most of these modern emigrants

to the West reach California. Between the middle of 1935 and May 1939 a full 300,000 persons of this class, or an average of above 6,000 a month, were counted entering the borders of that State alone, by automobile. More than nine-tenths are native American whites. A quarter had left Oklahoma, and another quarter had left Texas, Arkansas, and Missouri. Many of these refugees find their way to the cities, many return disappointed to the place of their origin, and many go again to the Pacific Coast. A large proportion, particularly of those from the four states named west of the Mississippi, pour into the agricultural sections seeking land. It is on the conditions of these who think to find opportunity in terms of the old frontier, that we present this section on our last West.

In California the old West is gone. Land is limited and dear. It was capitalized in the days of Chinese immigration on the expectation of continued ample supplies of cheap labor. It must be watered, and the cost of irrigation is high. Its price is in the hundreds of dollars per acre, beyond the reach of propertyless refugees from plantation, mid-continent, plains, or dust bowl. And the mysteries and hazards of fluctuating markets for highly commercialized crops confound the uninitiated.

The opportunity which the new emigrants find is more in the tradition of industry than of the pioneers on the prairies. In California the family-farm ideal embodied in the Homestead Act and established over a large part of the country, was never predominant. Its land pattern stems rather from large Spanish and Mexican grants, and from availability in the seventies and eighties of Chinese laborers ready to work cheaply and in gangs for entrepreneurs who brought water to land in large tracts. Thus agriculture in California became industrialized, and opportunity turns out to be not land, but jobs on the land.

The census of 1930 records that 37 percent of the large-scale farms of all types in the United States—those with gross income of approximately $30,000 or more—are in California. In that State are 41 percent of the large-scale dairy farms, 53 percent of the large-scale poultry farms, 60 percent of the large-scale truck farms, and 60 percent of the large-scale fruit farms of the United States. The same census reported that in Arizona and California, where less than three percent of the nation's cotton was produced, were 47 percent of the large-scale cotton farms. The number of these large-scale farms in California is less than 3,000 and they comprise hardly more than two percent of all farms in that State. But they produce nearly 30 percent of all California agricultural products by value.

The concentration in control of production is matched by concentration in control of employment. Of all California farms, 1.3 percent reported to the census of 1935 that they employ ten or more laborers, but together they employ more than one-third of all wageworkers. In Arizona the proportion working in gangs of ten or more rises almost to two-thirds.

Operation of the land by managers for absentee owners is extensive. One-quarter of all the cash used to employ labor on farms in Arizona and in California is spent by farm managers.

The conditions of laborers who serve highly industrialized, highly specialized, highly seasonal agriculture are not easy. The succession of sharp harvest peaks separated by hundreds of miles requires mobile workers ready to follow the crops. But the insistence of demand for their labor to tend perishable products has no balance in security of employment. In California the fluctuations which employ three laborers at the peak in the Fall leave two of them without jobs on farms in the Spring. Hire and fire as needed is the rule.

The life of the migrants is not a succession of vacation camping trips. Men, women, and children work. Earnings are low—perhaps $250 per worker on the average, and $450 per family. To even the poorest of these an automobile is a vital necessity and the cost of its operation cuts a large figure in the family budget. The car must be fed gasoline and oil to make the next harvest, or to get to and from the fields, and its wheels must be kept shod before the feet of the children. Squatters' camps on ditch banks and in the brush still survive despite stricter law enforcement and despite increasing efforts of large employers of labor to provide shelter. The Farm Security Administration of the United States Department of Agriculture has stepped into this situation, and has established a chain of sanitary camps and a medical service. But bad health conditions remain and malnutrition is rife among migrants and their children.

Although agriculture in California is industrialized, the protection of old-age insurance, unemployment compensation, and wage and hour laws is still denied to these workers on the land. Even relief, that lowest level of security, is precarious. The destitute and ill are shunted about from jurisdiction to jurisdiction and from agency to agency. Counties in California which depend on the coming of migrants to harvest their crops can hardly wait to get them out when work is over. At the conclusion of the pea harvest in one county the supervisors voted $2500 to fill the tanks of the pickers' cars with gasoline enough to get them into the next county to avoid having to feed them. The receiving county, resentful, sent word that if there is a repetition, the migrants will be turned back at the county line with guns.

The agricultural structure developed in California has its reflection in the character of the relations between employer and employed. A spokesman for agricultural interests asserts:

> The old-fashioned hired man is a thing of the past. . . . There is no place for him, and the farmer who does not wake up to the realization that there is a caste in labor on the farm, is sharing too much of his dollar with labor. . . . We are not husbandmen. We are not farmers. We are producing a product to sell. . . .

The pattern of labor conflict familiar in industry for decades has now spread to the land, but without the tempering effect which the growth of trade unions and long experience in bargaining collectively have exerted in industry.

The issues which arise between employer and employed rend the peace of the valleys. With the regularity of the seasons there is pressure on relief agencies to release clients to work at wages set by growers—if necessary, to "starve them out." Clergymen plead with growers to raise wages, and growers reply hotly that the clergy have "stepped out of their pulpits" and are "lining up on the side of the professional agitators." Merchants who give credit to strikers are pilloried and officials sworn to enforce the law impartially are directed in their duties. Citizen vigilantes by the hundred are deputized and armed with pick handles, and tear gas bombs explode on the highways.

Like eastern industrialists who fitted a stream of European peasants to their places in the mills, the growers in the West have utilized the influx of a succession of races from the Orient, Mexico, and the southern United States. The skills required are simple and readily learned. In 1910 when cotton first was grown in California, the *Imperial Valley Press* had misgivings over "the importation of hordes of undesirable people and the creation of troublesome social problems." But the pressure of demand for labor was strong, and within ten weeks the same paper carried the text of advertisements run in large dailies through the Cotton Belt:

> WANTED—1000 cotton pickers, for Imperial Valley, California. Wages, $1.00 per hundred pounds. . . . Colonists rates will be in effect on all railroads.

Testifying before a Congressional Committee in 1928 the manager of the Arizona Cotton Growers' Association recited that for 15 years his organization had been spending over $60,000 annually to recruit pickers from "all over the West, the Southwest . . . the southern sections of the United States," and elsewhere. Like the stream from a syphon, labor has continued to flow, aided when it slackens by vigilant watchfulness in the West.

When they arrive in the fertile valleys of the West, the migrants are the most ragged, half-starved, forgotten element in our population, needy, the butt of the jibes of those who look down on "fruit tramps," but with a surprising morale in the midst of misery, and a will to work. These people are not hand-picked failures. They are the human materials cruelly dislocated by the processes of human erosion. They have been scattered like the shavings from a clean-cutting plane, or like the dust of their farms, literally blown out. And they trek west, these American whites, at the end of a long immigrant line of Chinese, Japanese, Koreans, Negroes, Hindustanis, Mexicans, Filipinos, to serve the crops and farmers.

Far western agricultural communities depend upon prompt arrival of adequate supplies of mobile labor. But the development of normal relationships between citizen and community and between employer and employee, is not favored by constant movement. The laborer who comes to aid finds little welcome beyond the work he performs and the money he spends. "This rancher has us for two or three weeks, and then he's through with me. He knows me till he's through with me." "Residenters" look askance at nomads, and treat them as "outlanders." Children are stigmatized at school as "pea pickers." "Okies" and "Arkies" become terms of opprobrium, and citizens can imagine a lettuce strike as "a war between California and Oklahoma."

The link between South and West literally is human. For the South, the emigration of her people is like the escape of steam through a safety-valve. As rural problems assume a common form in both areas the bond becomes stronger. More and more the pattern of agriculture dominant in the West is spreading into the best cotton lands of the South. The forces which create large-scale, specialized farming dependent upon landless, propertyless, shifting families, are recasting our rural society. They are dissolving its bonds and compelling Americans, white and black, in the valleys of the West and the prairies and deltas of the South to "till the land of a man we don't know." We cannot escape these forces. We must face them.

MA BURNHAM

My father was a Confederate soldier. He give his age a year older than what it was to get into the army. After the war he bought 280 acres from the railroad and cleared it. We never had a mortgage on it.

In 19 and 20 the land was sold and the money divided. Now none of the children own their land. It's all done gone, but it raised a family. I've done my duty—I feel like I have. I've raised 12 children—6 dead, 6 alive, and 2 orphans . . .

*   *   *   *   *

Then all owned their farms. The land was good and there was free range. We made all we ate and wore. We had a loom and wheel. The old settlers had the cream. Now this hill land has washed. And we don't get anything for what we sell. We had two teams when this depression hit us. We sold one team—we had to to get by—and we sold 4 cows.

*   *   *   *   *

In 19 and 35 we got only 50 and 60 cents a hundred pounds for picking, and in 19 and 36 only 60 and 75 cents, and we hoe for 75 cents a day. Then the government reduced the acreage and where there was enough for two big families now there's just one. Some of the landowners would rather work the cotton land themselves and get all the government money. So they cut down to what they can work themselves, and the farming people are rented out. They go to town on relief—it's a "have to" case. Sharecroppers are just cut out.

Then the Lord taken a hand, and by the time He'd taken a swipe at it there was drought and army worm. I don't know whether that drought was the Devil's work or the Lord's work—in 3 days everything wilted.

Folks from this part has left for California in just the last year or so. My two grandsons—they were renters here and no more—went to California to hunt work. Those who have gone from here . . .

If you see my grandsons in California tell 'em you met up with Ma Burnham of Conroy, Arkansas.

June 28, 1938

DIRECTIONS: Some readers will ask, "If

these are the conditions, why do you not tell us what is being done to meet them, and what ought we to do?" The question is fair and deserves a candid reply.

Measures to relieve some acute distress have been taken, but beyond these little is done. In southern areas which families are leaving, government work projects (WPA) and loans to farmers for rehabilitation retard the exodus. Yet as 1939 opened, unknown numbers were leaving farm and plantation for towns nearby, and in May and June needy people, principally from rural sections, were being counted entering California at the rate of six thousand a month.

What these people want who have long made their living from the land is not relief. They want a chance for self-support. Yet often they are driven to relief. In areas of emigration direct relief is inadequate. Rates of from $4 to $12 per month per case which prevail are plainly insufficient from any point of view. And neither direct relief nor work relief are now administered selectively. We need administration which will distinguish between those who because of age or other reason should be anchored at home, and those younger families with strength and resilience, but facing blank futures, who should be released with some aid to find opportunity elsewhere.

In areas of destination general relief is makeshift and uncertain. Needy migrants fall afoul of settlement laws which make "residence" in state and county the requisite to receive help. States and counties vie with each other in their efforts to shed responsibility. As an inevitable expedient federal relief grants, largely of clothing and food, are given through the Farm Security Administration to sustain farm families who falter in this no man's land between the laws. We need comprehensive congressional action. We need federal aid to the states for general assistance as we now give federal aid for the aged, blind, and dependent children. This is necessary to diminish relief differentials between states of origin and states of destination, to equalize responsibility between them, and to care more surely and decently for families who seek opportunity by migration.

We do not yet know the magnitude of the problems we face in any of the areas where they are most pressing. The count of the influx over the California border is more than a clue to volume of movement, but there is no count of movement westward into other states, eastward through Arizona, southeastward into Florida, or northward to the cities. By the end of 1939 the results of studies under the Bureau of Agricultural Economics will furnish statistics of the migration to California, Oregon, Washington, and Idaho. But we must wait until 1941 for what the census can tell of this cleaning the land of people and filling the towns of the South.

Although we cannot now give figures for the dimensions of our problem, we do know that many hundreds of thousands of people already are caught in the toils of rural change, and that more hundreds of thousands face common fates. We know that continued or recurring agricultural depression or drought threatens the precarious foothold of many who still cling to the land. We know that more tractors were sold in 1937 than were in use on all farms of the country in 1920, and read in our magazines of more and better machines soon to reach market. By their very efficiency and advantage to some Americans on the land they spell tragedy for others. Surely the urgency of a national effort of first magnitude is not concealed by our lack of statistics.

What direction shall action take? It is plain that with advances in agricultural techniques the country requires fewer farmers rather than more. Probably nine-tenths of the commercial production of agriculture at this time is supplied by well under half of the nation's farms. Mechanization accentuates this. Further, the income of agriculture is not great enough to support more people adequately. About 21 percent of our gainfully employed workers are engaged in agriculture, but they received less than 9 percent of the national income in 1938. We do not believe, therefore, that more small subsistence farms afford suitable solution for those who are displaced from either agriculture or industry. The advance of the machine should not, and probably cannot be halted, but we do not favor denying participation in the advantages of a machine-produced standard of living to more farmers for subsistence.

The great reservoirs which the Reclamation Service is building in the West have given hope to some that upon their completion a new, if brief, era of homesteading will return. But the capacity of these projects to absorb settlers is limited. The Columbia Basin alone will ultimately irrigate 1,200,000 acres of land, or half the total of land to be irrigated by all of the Reclamation projects of the West. None of it will be ready for several years and the process of settlement will stretch out for a full generation. The United States Commissioner of Reclamation dashed effectively the hopes that new irrigation will resettle the refugees to the West when as early as January 1938 he said, "The Columbia Basin project, if it were finished at this time, would provide homes for less than half of the farm families already driven by drought from the Great Plains alone."

The real opportunity for large-scale absorption of the displaced must lie in the direction of industrial expansion, not in crowding them back onto the land where already they are surplus. Industrial expansion alone offers hope of permanently raising agricultural income to high levels and of employing at good standards the population produced but unneeded on the farms.

Awaiting industrial expansion, then, must those who are leaving the farms in tragedy be left to wander as day laborers on the face of the land, supported only by the mercy of relief. We do not think so. We believe that a number of measures can be taken to ameliorate their situation. Some of them already are under way, inaugurated by both public and private agencies. Something has been done by both growers and government to establish decent camps for migratory workers, especially in California, but only the beginning has been made. These shelters afford a basis upon which are built health, morale, and fitness for the exercise of citizenship under their new conditions.

Extensive construction of housing for agricultural workers in the good lands can also help those who are adrift in the country or crowded into the towns and intermittently drawn back to work on the land. For housing is not only shelter, but properly designed and coordinated with cooperative dairy, garden, and poultry production, it can be the source of income to supplement wages, an anchor of stability to families, and the foundation of a better community life.

One of the most serious and tragic aspects of the life of those who are loosened from the land is their ostracism from the communities in which they live and work. Nothing but good can result from the breakdown of the social barriers which are erected against them. The means of doing this are simple, and very human. We leave their details to the initiative and common humanity of the growers, to the members of small churches, to members of baseball teams, to teachers in the schools, and others who live in the communities where migrant people work.

In our concern over the visible and acute distress of dislocated people, we must not lose sight of the permanent farming organization which is being laid down. This grave question arises: After the sweep of mechanization, how shall our best lands be used—our southern plains, prairies, deltas, and our irrigated valleys of the West? Shall factory agriculture—our modern latifundia—prevail with its absentee owners, managers, day laborers, landless migrants, and recurrent strife? Or shall other patterns be sought for the relation of man to the land?

A very old American ideal, crystallized in the Homestead Act of 1862, holds that our land shall be farmed by working owners. But history has made serious inroads on this ideal. By 1935 tenancy had risen to 42 percent of all farms, and stood above 60 percent in many of the cotton states. Wage labor, standing at 26 percent of all persons gainfully employed in agriculture in 1930, reached 53 percent in Arizona and 57 percent in California. In order to preserve what we can of a national ideal, new patterns, we believe, must be developed.

Associations of tenants and small farmers for joint purchase of machinery, large-scale corporate farms under competent management with the working farmers for stockholders, and cooperative farms, are developments in the right direction. These devices conserve both the economies of machinery and organization and those elements of our national ideal which require security and a full share of the benefits for those who till the soil. They can be aided not only by government agencies which administer farm purchase and tenancy legislation, but also by private processors and others who now finance farm production.

In many places the old American family-size farm will long remain. But where it does not survive under the shock of change, new ways must be found if we are not to be confronted more and more with an organization of farm production which is harsh and already widespread. Our national effort must be well-planned, its support must be broadly based, and it must be long-sustained.

. . . We are now witnessing the outbreak of European war. Both agriculture and industry in this country will be stimulated. This may appear to some like a life preserver thrown to the displaced. But the acceleration of agriculture will be felt most in those very forms which now are displacing and limiting the opportunities of our people. Mechanization and industrialization on the land will spread. The false prosperity of war is no solution to the problems we describe. It is more likely to aggravate them.

THE EARTH

Here we bear our honors, here we exercise our
power, here we covet wealth, here we mortals
create our disturbances, here we continually
carry on our wars, aye, civil wars, even, and
unpeople the earth by mutual slaughter. And not
to dwell on public feuds, entered into by nations
against each other, here it is that we drive
away our neighbors, and enclose the land thus
seized upon within our fence; and yet the man
who has most extended his boundary, and has expelled the inhabitants for ever so great a distance, after all, what mighty portion of the earth
is he master of?

—Pliny, A.D. 77

ACKNOWLEDGMENTS: To SEVERAL photographers and institutions we are indebted for photographs we have included in our book. Their names, and the pages upon which their work appears are:

Farm Security Administration has made available from its files photographs taken by Dorothea Lange which appear on pages 11, 12, 15, 16, 17, 18, 22, 25, 29, 31, 33, 37, 39, 46, 48, 59, 63, 77, 78, 97, 107, 108, 110, 111, 112, 113, 114, 115, 116, 117, 119, 120, 122, 123, 125, 126, 127, 128, 129, 130, 132, 139, 140, 141, 142, 145.

Memphis Commercial-Appeal, 38
Oklahoma State Historical Society, 45
Arthur Rothstein for Farm Security Administration, 66, 102
J. H. Ward, Lamar, Colorado, 94
Hust Studio, Marysville, California, 136
Ron Partridge, 137
Horace Bristol, 138 upper
Otto Hagel, 138 lower

To my photographer-friends, Ansel Adams and Ron Partridge, I am indebted for the help they have given me.

DOROTHEA LANGE

We have used quotations from a number of writers, which we acknowledge as follows:

Rupert B. Vance, *Human Geography of the South* (Chapel Hill).
Arthur F. Raper, *Preface to Peasantry* (Chapel Hill).
Russell Lord, *To Hold This Soil* (U. S. Department of Agriculture).
M. L. Wilson and Ray Bowden, *Dry Farming in the North Central Montana Triangle* (Montana Experiment Station).
J. Russell Smith, *North America* (Harcourt, Brace).

PAUL SCHUSTER TAYLOR

American Farmers
and
The Rise of Agribusiness

Seeds of Struggle

An Arno Press Collection

Allen, Ruth Alice. **The Labor of Women in the Production of Cotton.** 1933

Bailey, L[iberty] H[yde]. **Cyclopedia of American Agriculture.** Vol. II: Crops. 1912

Bankers and Beef. 1975

[Bivins, Frank Jarris]. **The Farmer's Political Economy.** 1913

Blumenthal, Walter Hart. **American Indians Dispossessed.** 1955

Brinton, J. W. **Wheat and Politics.** 1931

Caldwell, Erskine and Margaret Bourke-White. **You Have Seen Their Faces.** 1937

Cannery Captives. 1975

Children in the Fields. 1975

The Commission on Country Life. **Report of the Commission on Country Life.** 1911

The Co-operative Central Exchange. **The Co-operative Pyramid Builder.** three vols. July 1926-January 1931

Dies, Edward Jerome. **The Plunger:** A Tale of the Wheat Pit. 1929

Dunning, N. A. **The Farmers' Alliance History and Agricultural Digest.** 1891

Everitt, J[ames] A. **The Third Power:** Farmers to the Front. 1907

The Farmer-Labor Party—History, Platform and Programs. 1975

Greeley, Horace. **What I Know of Farming.** 1871

Hill, John, Jr. **Gold Bricks of Speculation.** 1904

Howe, Frederic C. **Privilege and Democracy in America.** 1910

James, Will. **Cowboys North and South.** 1924

Kerr, W[illiam] H[enry]. **Farmers' Union and Federation Advocate and Guide.** 1919

King, Clyde L. **Farm Relief.** 1929

Kinney, J. P. **A Continent Lost—A Civilization Won.** 1937

Land Speculation: New England's Old Problem. 1975

Lange, Dorothea and Paul Schuster Taylor. **An American Exodus:** A Record of Human Erosion. 1939

Lord, Russell. **Men of Earth.** 1931

Loucks, H[enry] L. **The Great Conspiracy of the House of Morgan and How to Defeat It.** 1916

Murphy, Jerre C. **The Comical History of Montana.** 1912

The National Nonpartisan League Debate. 1975

Orr, James L. **Grange Melodies.** 1911

Proctor, Thomas H. **The Banker's Dream.** 1895

Rochester, Anna. **Why Farmers Are Poor.** 1940

Russell, Charles Edward. **The Greatest Trust in the World.** 1905

Russell, Charles Edward. **The Story of the Nonpartisan League.** 1920

Simons, A. M. **The American Farmer.** 1902

Simonsen, Sigurd Jay. **The Brush Coyotes.** 1943

Todes, Charlotte. **Labor and Lumber.** 1931

U. S. Department of Labor. **Labor Unionism in American Agriculture.** 1945

U. S. Federal Trade Commission. **Cooperative Marketing.** 1928

U. S. Federal Trade Commission. **Report of the Federal Trade Commission on Agricultural Income Inquiry.** 1938. three vols. in two

U. S. Senate Committee on Education and Labor. **Violations of Free Speech and Rights of Labor.** 1941. three vols. in one

Vincent, Leopold. **The Alliance and Labor Songster.** 1891

Wallace, Henry C. **Our Debt and Duty to the Farmer.** 1925

Watson, Thomas E. **The People's Party Campaign Book.** [1893]

[White, Roland A.]. **Milo Reno, Farmers Union Pioneer.** 1941

Whitney, Caspar. **Hawaiian America.** 1899

Wiest, Edward. **Agricultural Organization in the United States.** 1923

IF I COULD GET ME A PIECE OF LAND I'D GO TO DIGGIN IT WITH MY HANDS

TEXAS AND DON'T OWE OR OWN A THIN DIME BACK THERE ★ HE'S ALWAYS B

US ★ WE DRIED OUT THERE THREE YEARS HAND RUNNIN ★ THAT YEAR TH

TOR'S AS STRONG AGAINST US AS THE DROUGHT ★ WE MADE A DOLLAR WO

TRY—THEY RUN IT, WHAT I MEAN ★ THEM MEN THAT'S DOIN THE TALKIN

RENTERS OUT OF THEIR PLACES AND SCATTERING THEM ALL OVER ★ THEY DO

RIGHT SMART CHEAPER ★ THEY TAKE THE REDUCTION MONEY AND KICK US

WAS RAISED ON IT ★ ALL WE GOT TO START WITH IS A FAMILY OF KIDS ★

★ SEEMS LIKE PEOPLE HERE IS CRAZY ABOUT CALIFORNIA—THEY GO IN DROV

WORLD WAS SO WIDE. FATHER TO SON: NO, BUT I KNEW WHAT I WAS GOIN T

SIT BACK THERE AND LOOK TO SOMEONE TO FEED US ★ LIVIN A BUM'S LIFE S

A LIVIN EVEN THIS KIND OF A LIVIN BEATS STARVIN TO DEATH. BACK THERE

BLOWED OUT, EAT OUT, TRACTORED OUT ★ YESSIR, WE'RE STARVED STALLED

DON'T HAVE TO GO TO THE GOVERNMENT MAN FOR WHAT BREAD YOU EAT I

CHECK WHAT'S THAT BUT RELIEF? ★ WE AIN'T NO PAUPERS. WE HOLD OURSEL

CHANST TO MAKE AN HONEST LIVING LIKE WHAT WE WAS RAISED ★ SHE SAY

GITS DOWN TO YOUR LAST BEAN YOUR BACKBONE AND YOUR NAVEL SHAKES DI

HAVEN'T NOTHIN TO GO BACK TO ★ I COULDN'T DO NOTHIN IF I WENT BACK

HARM ★ WE TRUST IN THE LORD AND DON'T EXPECT MUCH ★ WE GOT EN

I'D BRING UP A BUNCH OF KIDS LIVING THIS WAY ★ I'VE WROTE BACK THAT

★ THEY SAY WE TOOK WORK CHEAP BUT YOU'VE GOT TO TAKE WORK CHEAP A

WANT YOU OUT OF THE WAY ★ I WAS BORN AND RAISED A 100 PERCENT AMER

MY FAMILY ★ WE LIVE MOST ANYWHERE IN GENERAL WHERE THERE'S WORK

WOULD ROT IF WE DIDN'T COME ★ BROTHER, HIT'S PICK SEVENTY-FIVE CEN

ELSE ★ MY BOYS ARE AMERICAN CITIZENS. IF WAR WAS DECLARED THEY'D H

CITIZENS BECAUSE WE MOVE AROUND WITH THE FRUIT TRYIN TO MAKE A LIVI